NuhQuim, The Little Red Puppy
A Star and Bumblebee Book

by
Jacqueline Paul
ÇOSINIYE Paul

Nuhquim, The Little Red Puppy
Copyright © 2022 by Jacqueline Paul

All rights reserved. No part of this publication may be reproduced, distributed, or transmitted in any form or by any means, including photocopying, recording, or other electronic or mechanical methods, without the prior written permission of the author, except in the case of brief quotations embodied in critical reviews and certain other non-commercial uses permitted by copyright law.

Tellwell Talent
www.tellwell.ca

ISBN
978-0-2288-7062-3 (Hardcover)
978-0-2288-7061-6 (Paperback)
978-0-2288-7063-0 (eBook)

For my step-daughter Sage, the Little-Big Sister, who's small and mighty, born and raised on her ancestral land in Tsartlip, British Columbia.

There was a family who lived in a field.
Fruits, flowers, and garlic the land did yield.
Sage-kitty, the tabby cat, marched about,
hiding from children who gave a loud shout!

The mum had a secret in the back of her car.
She'd plotted with Angel her neighbour not far,
from the field, by the forest, which the family did love,
who welcomed all pets, 'cause there were never enough.

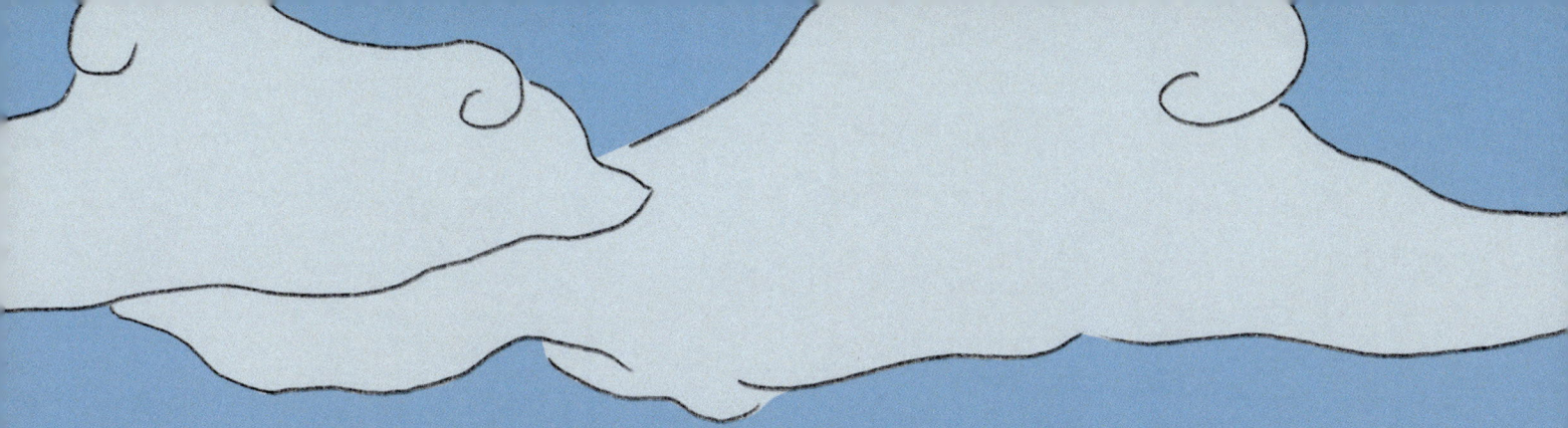

A red, fluffy bundle with a little bronze nose
was perched in her arms in an adorable pose.
With bright puppy eyes and a wiggly tail,
he ran through the grass like the wind through a sail.

Little-Big Sister was first on the scene.
His butterball body, so eager, so keen
to meet the young girl, whose arms opened wide
to cuddle and snuggle this pup to her side.

Tall-Little Brother was four and he thought……
he wanted to hold the new puppy A LOT!
When some sharp little teeth sank into his arm,
he yowled in great shock like a fire alarm!

Little-Big Sister was secretly glad
her brother ran off to tend to his scab
while she got to niggle and jiggle and bungle
with the happy new puppy in his grassy green jungle.

On stout little legs Baby-Sister did toddle,
grabbed hold of his fur, with intention to coddle,
wrapped strong, little arms around small, furry neck
and carried him clumsily up onto the deck.

This gave quite a chase
with sister and brother,
running in relay, heads
bobbing a-tother,
whilst puppy was happily
galloping around
the long rancher house,
like a goose from a hound.

The dad gave a scowl. How much more could he take?
Two running, one bleeding, one howling, for goodness' sake!
He gave a great bellow for all this to "Stop!"
They ground to a halt like an electrical shock.

With puppy dangling in Big Sister's arms,
the three young siblings succumbed to his charms:
his plump little body, his soft reddish fur.
They held him so tight, attached like a burr.

They fastened a collar and a short red leash.
They walked him around, in order to teach
this exuberant puppy, with fur on each limb,
that in their language they'd call him NuhQuim!

The End

P.S. Did you find Sage-kitty? How many times? Was it 10?
P.P.S. Did you find some stars and a bumblebee? Did you find the stars in the children's eyes?

Author's Note

I want to tell you about some things you may not know, like, this is the true story of our dog.

It's also a true story of our children. They were raised in a renovated house in the middle of a field with a beautiful forest behind it. They grew up on their ancestral land on the Tsartlip First Nation. Do you know where that is? If you don't, I'll tell you. It's on the Saanich Peninsula, just outside of Victoria, B.C. That's on Vancouver Island, in Canada, in case you are reading this from somewhere way far away.

My children have a First Nations father and a mother who was born in New Zealand and raised in Canada. They are W̱SÁNEĆ people. They are also known as Coast Salish or salt water people, because they are descendants of those who lived off the ocean and land. Today, the W̱SÁNEĆ live on four small reserves and their language, spoken for thousands of years (think of how many years that is!!) is called SENĆOŦEN. Their language is taught in an immersion program at ŁÁU,WELN̲EW̱ Tribal School and also at local schools.

My children's great-grandpa was the late Dave Elliott. He was born a long time ago, over a hundred years ago, in 1910! Things were a lot different then. As a boy, Dave travelled by canoe. His family fished and hunted and split their time between their winter and their summer camps, preparing for the next season. Dave was a very special man because he developed a way to write down the SENĆOŦEN language by producing a special alphabet that uses one letter to represent each sound. He used an old typewriter to do this. Do you know what a typewriter is? It's similar to but different than a keyboard. While a typewriter is like a small mechanical machine that hammers the imprint of letters onto a piece of white paper, a keyboard types your words onto a computer.

Our dog's name, NuhQuim, is derived from the SENĆOŦEN word for red, inspired by his fluffy red fur coat!

Do you want to learn another language, a very special language, the first language of this territory on Vancouver Island?

Here is Grandpa Dave Elliott's SENĆOŦEN alphabet!

W̱SÁNEĆ Language SENĆOŦEN Alphabet

A – Short "a" sound
Á – "ae" sound
Ā – Long "a" sound
B – Explosive "b" sound
C – Hard "c" sound
Ć – "ch" sound
₵ – "cw" sound
D – Explosive "d" sound
E – Short "u" as in "up"
H – regular "h" sound
I – Long "e" as in "ee"
Í – Long "i" as in "sigh"
J – Explosive "j" sound
K – Explosive "k" sound
K̶ – Explosive "kw" sound
Ḵ – Soft "k" sound
Ḱ – Soft "kw" sound
L – Regular "l" sound
Ł – Place tongue at roof of mouth while blowing "l"
M – Regular "m" sound
N – Regular "n" sound
Ṉ – "ng" sound
O – Short "o" as in "hop"
P – Regular "p" sound
Q – Hollow "qu" sound
S – Regular "s" sound
Ś – "sh" sound
T – Regular "t" sound

T̶ – "ts" sound
Ṯ – "tl" sound
Ŧ – "th" sound
U – "oo" as in "boo"
W – Regular "w" sound
W̱ – "w" with soft blowing sound rounding lips
X – SENĆOŦEN "x" sound
X̱ – SENĆOŦEN "x" sound while rounding lips
Y – Regular "y" sound
Z – Regular "z" sound
s – Regular "s" sound indicates possessive

The SENĆOŦEN language is considered the first birthright of W̱SÁNEĆ people. It was the way the Creator first spoke to the ancestors. Within the language is the pattern of how to live a W̱SÁNEĆ way of life, a framework that should be followed throughout time to maintain the Creator's gifts from one generation to the next. It is a sacred responsibility that was given to W̱SÁNEĆ people.

The orthography, developed by PENÁĆ, late Dave Elliott, is used today in the W̱SÁNEĆ School Board's SENĆOŦEN LENO̱NET SCUL,ÁUTW̱
- SENĆOŦEN Immersion Survival School.
Here are some words that you can say in SENĆOŦEN!

Can you say my daughter's name? ȻOSINIYE
It is: cwah-see-nee-yu

Thank you, HÍSW̱ḴE
And Goodbye for now, HÍYÁ,ȻE

Glossary

ḴE,ḴE,IŁĆ
Arbutus

TŦE ŚW̱OḰE / ŦE ŚW̱OḰE
Brother / Sister

SEMSEMÍYE
Bumblebee

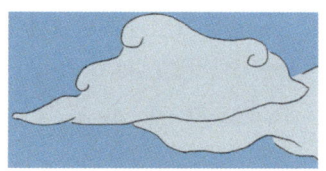
ŚNOU,ES
Clouds

X̱E,ON̠
Crying

LELEJ,IŁĆ
Dandelion

ŦE LOT̠
Eldest Sister

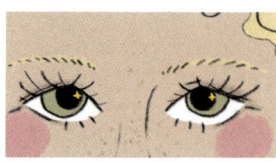
ḴE,ḰI,LEN
Eyes

MÁN
Father

JSÁ
Fir Tree

HI,LEĆ
Happy

ŚW̱ KIDE E TT̵E SPEL₭IT̸E
Honeysuckle
(swing of the spirits)

W̱ITEN̲
Jumping

TÁN
Mother

T̸IT̵EŁ SN̲Á,NET
Mountain

N̲EKSEN
Nose

NEĆIM
Red

ĆEN,NIN̲ET̸ T̵
Run

ȻOSEN
Star

ĆEĆI,NES
Teeth

SNEPET
Sternly talking to someone
DEJOȻES
To look angry

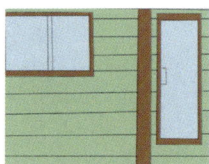
ŚQENOSEN̲
Window

E HÁ,EĆ /TŦE SEÁĆEN
Youngest Sister/Younger Brother

Thank you kindly to ȻOSINIYE Elliott and the support of the SENĆOTEN Language Council for their time in doing the language translations and the use of their SENĆOTEN Language alphabet. HÍSW̱ḴE

Manufactured by Amazon.ca
Bolton, ON

27915729R00021